First Ladies

Barbara Bush

Jennifer Strand

Launch!
An Imprint of Abdo Zoom
abdopublishing.com

abdopublishing.com

Published by Abdo Zoom, a division of ABDO, PO Box 398166, Minneapolis, Minnesota 55439.
Copyright © 2019 by Abdo Consulting Group, Inc. International copyrights reserved in all countries.
No part of this book may be reproduced in any form without written permission from the publisher.
Launch!™ is a trademark and logo of Abdo Zoom.

Printed in the United States of America, North Mankato, Minnesota.

052018
092018

THIS BOOK CONTAINS
RECYCLED MATERIALS

Photo Credits: Alamy, AP Images, George Bush Presidential Library and Museum, Getty Images, Shutterstock

Production Contributors: Kenny Abdo, Jennie Forsberg, Grace Hansen, John Hansen

Design Contributors: Dorothy Toth, Neil Klinepier

Library of Congress Control Number: 2017960618

Publisher's Cataloging-in-Publication Data

Names: Strand, Jennifer, author.

Title: Barbara Bush / by Jennifer Strand.

Description: Minneapolis, Minnesota : Abdo Zoom, 2019. | Series: First ladies |
    Includes online resources and index.

Identifiers: ISBN 9781532122828 (lib.bdg.) | ISBN 9781532123801 (ebook) |
    ISBN 9781532124297 (Read-to-me ebook)

Subjects: LCSH: Bush, Barbara 1925-, Biography--Juvenile literature. | Presidents' spouses--United
    States--Biography--Juvenile literature. | First ladies (United States)--Biography--Juvenile literature.

Classification: DDC 973.9280 [B]--dc23

Table of Contents

Introduction

Barbara Bush was a First Lady of the United States. Her husband George H. W. Bush was the 41st US president.

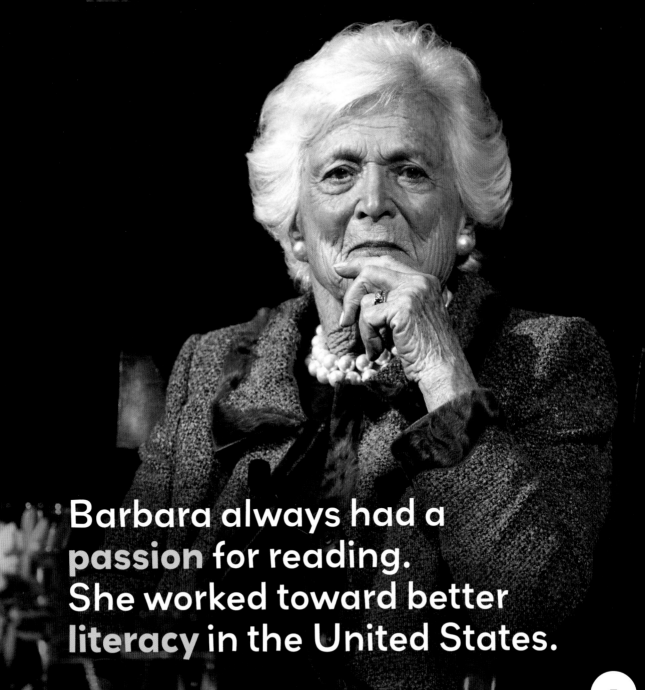

Barbara always had a **passion** for reading. She worked toward better **literacy** in the United States.

Early Life

Barbara Pierce was born on June 8, 1925 in New York City. She grew up in Rye, New York.

She met George H. W.
Bush when she was 16.
They were married a few
years later in 1945.

She left college early to take care of their family and home.

George H. W. Bush became vice president in 1981. Barbara traveled abroad often. She met with many foreign leaders.

She spoke in more than 60 countries and in all 50 states.

First Lady

Barbara Bush
became First Lady
in 1989.

That same year she created the Barbara Bush Foundation for Family **Literacy**. It worked to get families to read together.

She visited schools and read to children.

After being First Lady, Bush focused on her family. She continued to give speeches and **volunteer**.

Barbara is **honest** and friendly. She is known as "everybody's grandmother."

Quick Stats

Barbara Bush

Born: June 8, 1925

Birthplace: New York City, New York

Husband: George H. W. Bush

Years Served: 1989–1993

Known For: Bush was a First Lady of the United States. She worked for greater literacy for families in the United States.

Key Dates

1925: Barbara Pierce is born on June 8.

1945: Barbara marries George H. W. Bush on January 6.

1981–1989: Barbara Bush is Second Lady while Ronald Reagan is president.

1989–1993: Barbara Bush is the First Lady. George H. W. Bush is the 41st president.

1989: Bush starts the Barbara Bush Foundation for Family Literacy.

2001: Bush's son George W. Bush becomes president.

Glossary

honest – fair and truthful.

literacy – the ability to read and write.

passion – a strong feeling of excitement for something or about doing something.

volunteer – to offer to give one's time to help others without being paid.

Online Resources

For more information on
Barbara Bush, please visit
abdobooklinks.com

Learn even more with the
Abdo Zoom Biographies database.
Visit **abdozoom.com** today!

Index